The Haunting

poetry & prose
MELISSA M. COMBS

"Weeping may endure for a night,
but joy cometh in the morning."
-Psalms 30:5

The Haunting

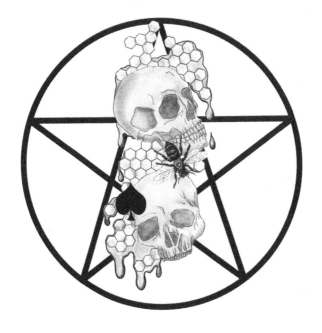

poetry & prose

MELISSA M. COMBS

"If all else perished, and he remained, I should still continue to be; and if all else remained, and he were annihilated, the universe would turn to a mighty stranger."

- Catherine Heathcliff, *Wuthering Heights*

Dedicated to: *The very hands holding this book.*

Haunted, though you may be, for a season in time...
it is merely a preparation — a divine intervention,
readying you for your very first footsteps, as you will soon
enter your heaven on earth.

May the experience of this book bring you great comfort,
as you learn that your highs and your lows were always
meant to be a part of the journey. In between the pages, you will
notice a spike in belief, love, and positive feelings, only to on the next
page or so, notice a drastic free fall once more, into the pit.
Embrace it. Accept it. Learn from it —
for we do not stay down forever.

Happy haunting,
Melissa.

It hurts,
it haunts,
and then it
heals.

I'll admit,
our story felt more
nightmare than fairytale,
but at least it taught me
what it meant to really have feelings —
both terrifying and beautiful,
gut wrenching, whole hearted,
soul-freeing feelings.

He said, "your mind is brilliant."

I laughed, "my mind is nothing more
than haunted; my words, nothing more
than attempted exorcisms."

I knew that *loving* you was dangerous,

but losing you was lethal.

In pain and in pieces,
I dipped my fingers into
my blood and still I wrote
for you and of our nightmare
that we called l o v e.

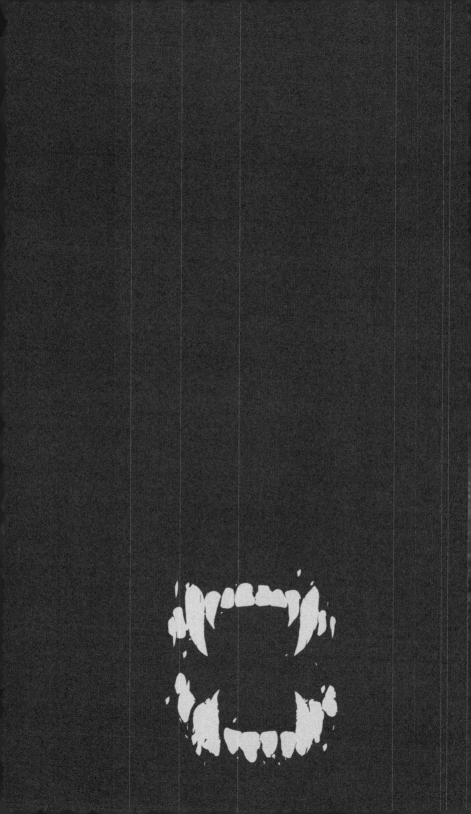

It was only a bite,
I remind myself.
And what you're feeling for him
is not *l o v e* ,
but the remnants of his venom coursing
steadily through your veins.

For those of you new
to *love*, just remember this
so as not to be naive...
the bite of *love* can be merciless
and its hunger, insatiable.

And I do not care what anyone
tells you,
you cannot control who
you fall in *love* with,
nor can you control how
long you *love* them once
they are gone.

Just *love* at your own risk, okay?

Because one bite is all it takes
for you to be left hollow ribbed
and starving for more.

The Haunting

Smile, they say.
But they don't know that I am only half alive —

that *l o v i n g* you nearly killed me.

The Haunting

20

As I hand over my *l o v e* as a holy sacrifice,
I watch you exercise your silence as the
drawing of a sword.
Staring at my heart and visualizing its
very last beat as an atonement for
your sins.

Why all of these games?

Don't you know that in love, we come alive,
and in vein pursuit, we so foolishly die?

In one entity,
I found both a dream
and a nightmare;
a desire
and an unwanted tie —

and because of this,
still I curse the day
that we met,
and long for the day
that we may meet again.

My life as your sacrificial lamb is spent —
every drop of blood from within me, spilt.

And the truest pain was not in dying,
but in knowing that my blood was not
enough to save you.

Somewhere in between
wishing to be possessed by you
and wishing to save you,
thats where I began to lose myself.

Tell me once and for all that I am nothing
more than a victim placed under your spell.

At least then I will be left with hope.
For it is written that all spells, no matter
their strength, *can* be broken, but that *l o v e*,
even unrequited, cannot.

You uttered the word "always," and then stood their
idly, as if we had all of forever before us.

And I wanted to believe you,
god did I want to believe you.
But the problem was that
your inconsistency had already sent my viewpoint
of a forever into an arising state of disbelief.

The Haunting

I guess I became a bit of a masochist when I
learned that the only way left to feel you was
through the memories
and the pain.

When the teeth are gone,
the skin will heal itself.
The hardest part is removing
the venom,
because that
you must find a way
to do on your own.

No one ever tells you
how hard that process really is,
or even how long it will take…
only that it is both possible
and worth it in the end.

(And which it is)
But holy fucking hell…
does the extraction burn.

My dreams of him were the bricks,
our memories, the windows,
and his idle promises,
the barb-wired fence
that kept me
locked in.

And while it may have
taken me some time
to learn,
eventually I did —
that this was not *l o v e*
that I was in…

this was an asylum.

I noticed that when I tried to hold on to you,
it was not my arms that I began to lose,
but more precious, my soul —
bit by bit, piece by piece...
until you and everything
that you were, was nearly all
that was left of me.

The Haunting

To him,
I was bound,
not by the negligent knots and loopholes
of an ordinary soul tie,
but by well thought out and strategic ties.

I was blood red wrists,
anticipation flenches,
and shivers all down my spine.

I was 'yes sir,'
'do as you wilt,'
and 'I am yours, for all of time.'

To be in pursuit of you
is to repetitively face the unknown.

It is walking the shadowed valley,
wishing for the mercy of a compass,
or as a last resort, a blindfold...
only for my eyelids to be
forcefully held open by the anguish,
as I relentlessly search my way out.

The Haunting

You can run, they tell me,
but you can never hide.

Yet still, I am in the closet —
pitch black.
I am under the covers —
stack of ten.
I am underground —
hurricane shelter…
and all I can do is cry.

I fear he has become a part of me,
and they are right…
there is *nowhere* left to hide.

There is nothing wrong with you
for falling in *l o v e* with what once
haunted you.

If anything, I'd say that
you're just a little braver than most —
that you have a little more faith than most —
that you were willing to dive deeper
than most.

For everything
in life,
we abide by a
law.

Ours, the law of
magnetism.

A bee to flowers;
the moon's placement
in the sky.

Some things are always
destined to be —
you and I.

In *l o v i n g*
you,
somehow
I forgot what
made myself
so unique —

praising your
existence
as the flower,
while failing
to acknowledge
that without me
working tirelessly
to extract your
nectar,
the two of us
would never
come
to know *honey.*

The Haunting

And now I've got your voice
inside of my head.

But even it won't tell me why
you're still lingering inside of me,
long after you've left.

List of things that terrify me more than dying:

1. Living my one and only life, haunted by the ghost of you, feeling as though I am already dead.

And I guess I am scared to find out that my insomnia
is nothing more than thoughts of you;
that this heaviness inside of my chest, my panic,
is really just my fear that our time is truly up.
That the reason that I can't eat some days is because
I still can't stomach the loss of you.

That I am more than sick,
but *l o v e* sick —
a kind of sickness that has yet to land a cure.

An open letter to my nameless lover:

I refuse to allow my body to serve as your host anymore —
not in this lifetime. not anymore. not knowing
that you are still very much alive and well. that you chose
to walk away. that there was someone else out there.
that in your mind, I was replaceable.

Since you could not *l o v e* me,
what makes you think that you have any right to haunt me?

The Haunting

And now that I am drained,
I realize that
you were more vampire
than you were man.

And I was more prey,
than I ever was *l o v e d*.

On the day that you realize
you have finally lost me,
know that it was my last attempt
at *l o v i n g* you —

to finally rid you of me;
to give you the chance, for the
first time, since meeting me...
to just breathe.

Every highway leads to you;
every skyline reminds me of you.
As the lines of the lanes blur,
the memories resurface and flood
my mind.

And there you are again.
There are our memories;
our victories, even.
But mainly, our tragedies.

The Haunting

I waited for you,
the one who left me alone
and lost at sea,
for so many days and so many nights,
longing to be held
by the very hands
that were drowning me.

And I think that maybe
that's just what we as humans do
when we believe that we have
little to live for.

We live for anything —
even those that
seek to destroy us.

And you *almost* did.
You *almost* destroyed me.

The Haunting

I wonder, who is weaker,
the frail and withering leaves of autumn,
or the strong and sturdy tree,
powerless to hold the leaves?

And too I wonder,
who is weaker, myself for
falling to my decay,
or you, for mercilessly releasing me?

Maybe it is only when the weight
of their memory begins to feel
as heavy and as grim as death
do we wish to finally let them go.

Maybe you weren't *love*.
And maybe you weren't my knight and shining
armor after all.

Maybe you were nothing more than a
coward of a warlock casting careless *love* spells.

What is earth but a
temporary dwelling place to learn
of the one in which we were
created for?
To *love* extensively,
and to long exhaustively;
where anticipation builds and our
ruthless hunger grows.

Though your absence took
every part of me —
body, mind, and soul…
it is not the final show for me.

For I too, on the third day,
shall rise and be made whole.

The Haunting

She had grown too tall
for him to care for.

She was a rose,
left there to die
by a very small man.

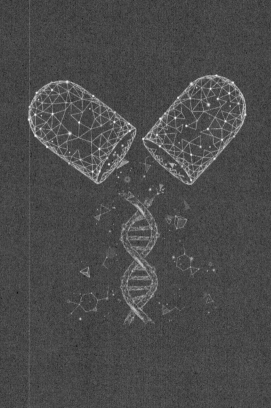

Before I knew it he had simultaneously become
both my ecstasy and a heart shattering misery;
the poison that I would reach for
with sweaty palms and a racing heart.

And now I am deep breaths and heavy shivers,
feigning like I would take my last breath
for just one more hit.

When he is in reach,
I am weightless — no longer bound
to earth's gravity, but in union
with the galaxy,
her stardust and all of her glory.

Yet when he is gone,
he is my cold and grey come down,
and the various colors draining
from my eyes.

He is both my poison
and my antidote;
the lowest of my lows,
and the highest of my highs.

The Haunting

The Haunting

We are told that it is a sin to want what is not ours.

But I do wonder,
how vast is the mercy for those
of us under *l o v e ' s* spell?

Nothing haunts us more
than the ghost of a lost *l o v e*,
not by death,
but by choice.

Where might I find the you
that I once knew?
Because right now I search frantically
behind dark and loveless eyes,
without a trace of evidence
that you were ever even mine.

As children we tend to develop these fears —
fears that our parents will oftentimes tell
us are unrealistic;
that have a one percent probability of ever
even happening.
Like being haunted by ghosts,
being eaten alive,
or becoming possessed.

And I just wish that their reassurance would
have been true.
But the cruel and bleak truth to it all is that
maybe I am the one percent —
haunted by you,
eaten alive by your decision to leave,
and possessed with a burning desire
to find my way back to you.

The Haunting

I was warned,
"the devil will send you that in
which you desire the most."

And there you were,
in all of your dark
an angelic glory.

And there I fell,
irrevocably in *l o v e ;*
a servant at your feet.

The Haunting

When I awaken each and every morning, the question is,
will we ever meet again?

When I stumble across an old photo of
you and I, the question is,
will we ever meet again?

When I hear or see your name,
will we ever meet again?

And even when I am asleep and my mind is at rest,
still, the question is,
will we ever meet again?

I can only hope and pray that your
intentions were never to haunt me —
that these things, they just happen
when you experience
both *l o v e* and loss.

But why are these memories more like
night-terrors, than a blissful re-visiting?
Why is your face grey,
and your voice cold, when we do finally
speak?
I had hoped to look back on us in peace;
not this. Where all that lies between is
so chilling and unforgivably bleak.

Why haunt me?
Why not just release me?

The Haunting

A tale as old as old as time —
union of the lion and the lamb;
the mortal and the immortal;
the beast and his beauty.

I must only remind myself
that leading up to the grand
finale is rarely ever pretty.
It is here that I
must absolutely
stand strong in my faith
in restoration,
and new beginnings.

I once believed that falling in *l o v e*
was to be light and
harmless.
but having fallen for you,
I now know the truth.

Falling in *l o v e* must sometimes be
the equivalence
of an angel losing
their wings;
a slow and painful
descent
to hell —

so that in falling,
we might finally
teach ourselves
to fly.

I'm no where near healed
from you,
and I know that I am
still parcels away
from reaching heaven,
having landed myself
in hell.

And I may be countless
trials and errors away
from finding
the light...

but it sure beats
where I was when
you first left me.

The Haunting

I must know, was there any part of you that cared?

Or was your heart too consumed
by the fire,
your mind too enslaved to it's ego,
and your soul too indebted to the game?

Allow me to forget you;
loosen the noose from
around my throat.

If not for me,
than for your own
name.

My *l o v e* for you has
always been
sink or swim;
do or die.

It is not timid at heart,
nor does it cower
to fear.

Never will it
find pleasure in
your fleeting descents.

It does not wish for you,
what has become of me.

It is unfailing and unwavering;
a truthful flowering;
raw
l o v e,
forever,
without end.

They say that heaven
is where our souls have
been tied.

But in our case,
I believe them to have
been tied in a house,
haunted and abandoned;
a connection
that was never tended to;
dried up,
forgotten,
and left to painfully die.

I have never been so sleepless,
nor have I hungered for another,
as I have,
for you.

This mind of mine is now nocturnal,
and this heart, a sleep-walker, when you
are no where near.

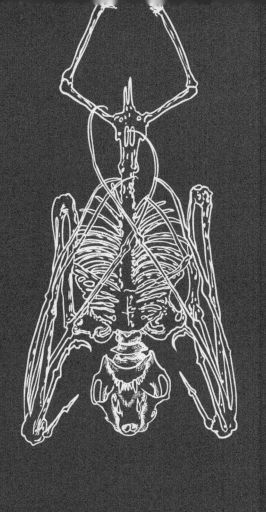

I fell into you like a rock skipping the surface
of a river —
wishing to flow amongst you,
sinking to the bottom of you.
Your waves,
skimming past me,
always somewhere else you had to be,
but rarely resting along side me.

The Haunting

To have and to hold
you for all of forever,
I was willing to place your soul
inside of my body —
become you,
so that I may never
again have
to long for or miss you.

But as time has passed,
I have thankfully learned
that is not *l o v e.*

Therefore,
live alongside me;
merge with me,
and then freely roam
this earth,
as your own separate entity.

So long as you vow to always
come back for me.

If it does come
to be truth,
that you are not
to be mine
in this lifetime,
then at least
I will know,
without question,
that this world is
not my home.

The Haunting

If you came back to me now,
all of the pieces of me that I tried
so desperately to bury,
I would boldly resurrect.

And if you still did not desire me,
then I would, once and for all,
bury the story of you and I.

But never again —
never again
will I bury myself.

It was less that I was shy,
and more that I was speechless
in the center of your gravity.

You said,
"let your walls down,"
mistaking my reverent awe of you
as walls — an awe that I knew
would never cease,
so long as I lived.

So as you walked away,
one thing remained the same —
my awe of you,
only now,
from so far away.

I guess
the silver-lining is this,

nothing scares me
the way that it used to...
not having lost you.

Having lost you,
I faced one my life's greatest fears —
to find heaven on earth,
only to then have it ripped
viciously from within my reach.

The Haunting

If you leaving was you strengthening
me, then consider it a mission complete.

For I am now colder than before,
wiser than before,
stronger than before;
resilient to the core.

Yet still I am lacking *l o v e.*
and what is strength
without *l o v e ,*
but the creaking of a rusty gate?

They tell me that this will get easier
with time —
this being the loss of you.
But they don't know that time has
other plans for me;
that everyday that I am without you,
the longing increases,
the pain remains,
and my *l o v e* for you grows.

They mean well,
I know that they do.
I just have to remind myself that
not everyone experiences what I
have experienced with you.

3   **6**

l o v i n g you opened me to the secrets
of life.

9

Nothing would ever be the same,
this I knew.
Where others, by sheer luck,
had made their way into small
portions of my heart,
he had effortlessly nestled his way
into every cell of my body,
every corner of my mind,
and every fragment of my spirit.

Life as I had previously known it
to be, was never to exist again.

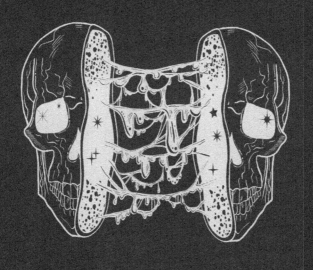

I can't make sense of this.
I'm home-sick, now that you are gone.

But you are no home.
I'm not even certain that you are human.
You're cold.
Calculating.
Distant.
Cruel.

Why have I made such darkness my home?

I've lost many
people over the
span of my life,
and in the years
to follow their loss,
the memory of them
would of course
reappear from
time to time.

But the memory of you?
It is impossible
for something
to reappear,
that has never,
even for a moment,
left.

The Haunting

You couldn't just be another life
that I easily left behind, could you?

You had to become the question left
unanswered —
the question that I would form like a
thirst formed in the desert;
a drink I would beg of to fall from the sky...
so dry at the mouth that my screams
would soon after run silent.

My lifeblood;
My heart's synchronistic beat;
My *everything.*

May the death of my former self
always be tribute to you —
the way that I persisted to rebirth,
despite my fears and my failings.

I died unto myself a thousand times
to find my way back to you.

I don't have the words
to describe the way in which
I am feeling —
only that the pain is a solid
twelve,
and my tolerance,
a ten;
only that your *l o v e* is the ocean,
and I have been introduced before
learning how to swim.

The Haunting

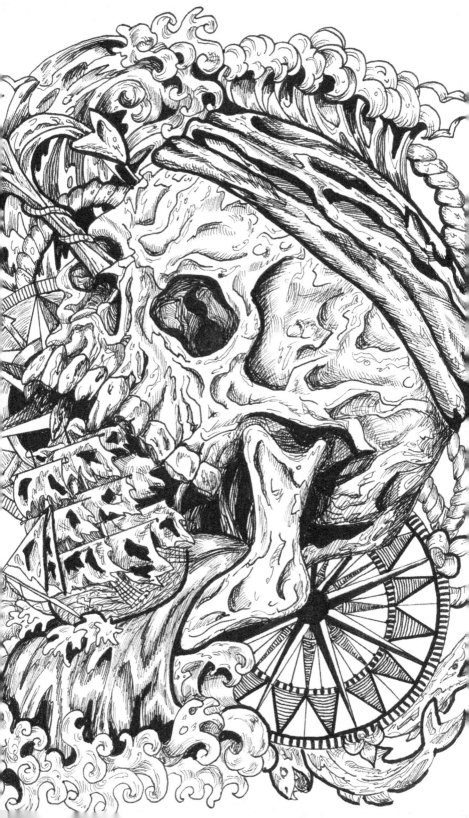

I have pondered
innumerable times
the likelihood of this
l o v e
being a spell.
and in doing this,
I have learned just
how deep I am in.

For even if it were
a spell,
I would wish not for it
to break.

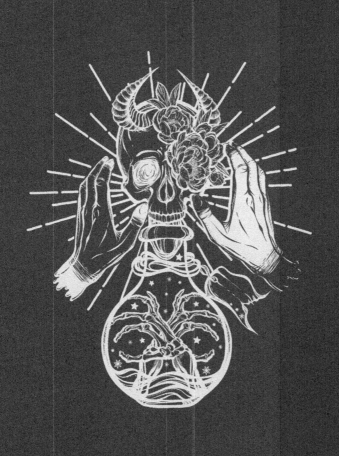

I want to believe that your intent
was only to fortify me,
to test me,
to break me,
and then to restore me.

Yet the weight of losing you
is currently too heavy for brisk,
light,
and hopeful feelings,
such as these.

Maybe once more time has
passed and the weight has
finally lifted,
then I may,
once and for all,
with clear eyes, *see.*

I am told that this is just life —
the fate of all,
and that I am by no means
exempt.

How self-righteous I must be
to dream that fate would handle
me with any more leniency.
Heartbreak finds it's way to all,
they say.

But to them I respond,
it is not that I am
holier-than-thou,
only that I am a dreamer,
and that in these dreams
of mine,
I have stumbled upon the
secret, and that secret is
belief.

(From me, heartbreak must soon flee.)

The Haunting

True *love* is to know grief, at some
point or another.
For I have never met another that
has *loved* and lost,
yet wished never to have met,
having lost.

And that is because at some point or another,
the beauty of *love* chokes out the
grief of loss.

The Haunting

Meeting you
ignited a fire-like
fever inside of me.

Losing you
sent me roaming a
cold and foreign world,
in search of even
the faintest of sparks
to bring me back to life.

The Haunting

I may never know the forces that
brought
us together,
plotting soon after
to rip us apart.
Yet, nor do I care to.

All I have left to give to this entity,
is pity.

How low to join together and then separate
something so other-worldly and beautiful;
something as rare as you and I.

The Haunting

Once upon a time,
I searched for the answers
as I studied relentlessly
the patterns of
the stars.
But I fear that time has
since then depleted
my energy,
and all I have left
is the ability to
wish upon them
instead.

For you.
For us.
For mercy.

No energy left to work,
only to wish,
for now.

The Haunting

If a coin is permitted to have
both heads and tails,
then i wish to forever feel you,
yet I wish the feeling to abruptly cease.

And if god may exhibit both *l o v e*
and grace,
all consuming fire and rage,
then I wish to admit that you
are both my most beautiful source
of peace,
and yet my greatest source of pain.

I am a bizarre creation, I will admit —
the way that I repetitively condemn my pain,
yet run headlong in his direction,
the very moment that he calls my name.

We are the strange and the unusual
l o v e story;
a timeless box office hit;
the kind of *l o v e* that people write
stories of, fixate upon, and secretly
dream of one day living;
a story worthy of capturing it's audience,

And capture,
we surely will.

The Haunting

If the absence of your memory
promised the absence of pain,
why is it that I am still stuck
at the crossroads of this?

My left foot begging me to swiftly
turn to run away;
my right,
in synchrony with my heart,
begging of me to stay.

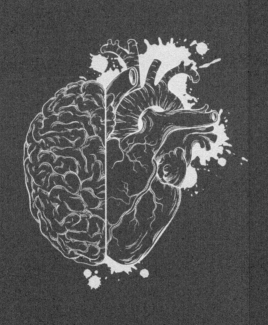

My *l o v e* for you never sleeps —
like a haunted house,
empty of flesh,
yet the stirring of
a thousand generations
of ghosts
living on inside.

I fear I am now a home that
will never find its rest.

It's beautiful,
yet a tragedy, all the same,
to learn that some ghosts...
they never leave us.

My mind oftentimes tortures
me with claims that you are
moving on, so effortlessly,
without me.
Yet my soul reminds me that
your higher being
will *always* remember me,
always yearn for me,
and *always* *l o v e* me.

Who was I to go on
living a lie —
pretending that you
had not already declared
dominion over
my heart;
pretending that this kind of
l o v e was ever going to fade?

All of these claims of moving on,
and giving you up, they are all lies.

The Haunting

The Haunting

Torturing as it may be
to somehow always find you
in my mind,
I find comfort and beauty
knowing that it is the one place
you and I shall never die.

You want an accurate description of *l o v e* ?

It is the fire of all fires,
forever and always,
raging on, growing in strength,
and ever duplicating in size.

Its flames violently catching the wind,
is its reminder to us, that its pursuit is
as wild as it is relentless.
And the smoke that it produces,
is its laughter to all that wish
to scuff it out.

If only meeting you carried a message of
warning,
like a doctor moving in with the
administration of a shot.
"This is only going to sting for a second."

Only yours would state,
"the pain could last a lifetime."

If only you knew how aware I am
of the poison I have been administered
by you —
like Jesus eating alongside Judas,
how much I was willing to take;

how much I *love* and pray for you,
despite all of your hate.

The Haunting

You coiled yourself around my heart,
leaving no room left for me to *love* another
the way that I *love* you.

One day,
I will thrive like never before —
my heart,
as the seed;
my words,
as the water;
my belief,
as the soil.

And there, the most breath taking
flowers that I will ever grow,
they will bloom.

But for now,
I am simply just doing my best
to survive this life without you.

The Haunting

L o v e another, if you must;
I will always see to it that you are free.

Only promise me one thing...
that you will never *l o v e* another
the way that you *l o v e* me.

Wherever this life may take us,
let us vow these two things of our *love,*
to keep it rare and to keep it alive.

Maybe to mourn someone
is to be with them still.

I always said that it was all or nothing
for me, didn't I?

And now, reduced to the nothing
that I have for so long vowed,
you see my *l o v e* for the depths of
what it is; what it has always been.

Pledged to inflate your ego
at the expense of sacrificing
my own self...
because all I've ever wanted was
to see you smile...
even if the smile were a little sinister
and bent.

It was as if i had been watched
and studied
my entire life;
prepped and primed
for him and only him —
my every wish,
my every prayer,
and my deepest desires
existing fully and woven
intricately into the details
of this one man.

And as terrifying as it was to admit,
I knew that I didn't so much as
stand a chance.

I am unsure how I will —
the details and the
technicalities of pulling
myself out of the
trenches of you.

But I know that I am
very much capable,
and that if I have to
fight tooth and nail,
I will.

I *will* survive you.

The Haunting

January 1st;
a new year —

A new year,
yet nothing more
than the lingering
of the golden years
passed.
Nothing more than
an intensified longing
for a home that we are once
more made painfully aware
that we have yet to find.

Raised glasses and
shouting "Happy New Year,"
to hide our silent screams
for the *l o v e* that we
begged to never lose.

(The after math of you)

When you left me,
it sent me searching
for ways to
tap into the astral plane.

*What other choice
did I have?*

I wasn't going to lose
you any more than
I had to.

They say that when you lose
someone that you *l o v e*,
they forever live on inside of you.

And while I am grateful for this,
this alone will not sustain me for
long.

Soon you must, again, be mine.

If you are to leave,
you must in turn accept that you are leaving
behind a piece of yourself.
Therefore, you too, must carry the burden
of navigating our way out of the complexity
of this hell.

They see you for your acts,
where as
I see you for the soul behind your acts.

For you, they merely hold lust;
for you, I have and will always
hold Philos, Eros, and Agape.

And if tomorrow you were to awaken
as a stranger even to yourself,
still I would know you,
l o v e you,
and fight to restore you.

(Lust gives up; *l o v e* endures.)

There was something about the way
that the universe knew of my never ending
thoughts of him,
my tireless pleas,
and its constant withholding from me...

something about it,
so cold and calculating.

Every cell within my blood,
flows through me,
effortlessly spelling out your name.

Sometimes I feel that my
body is more yours than it ever
was mine.

From the angels,
I could have sworn that I heard
them say,
"Until he is but a distant memory."

And that day was one of the hardest
for me...
because in that moment,
I learned that I was in fact
a stranger to this world.

For even the angels had failed
to understand my heart
and the depths of my *l o v e* for him.

And while I knew that I was strong enough
to let him go,
I had already vowed to all things holy,
to fight and to endure;
to *l o v e* and to call us home.

Though I have far more life to live,
and wisdom to acquire,
I am at least confident in this —
l o v e is not weakness,
nor is it madness,
as some might claim.

It is merely a gift to be received
by those of us that are
brave at heart.

The Haunting

I would write you
out of my mind if I could —
every word would erase
more and more of you.

And that very last pencil stroke,
a beautiful ending to my
life's most painful story.

You were fearful of letting
me shine too bright —
thought I may cast you
as the moon.

Darling,
I only wished to share the sky,
spending forever next to you.

The Haunting

You were brave to even
describe your feelings for
me as *l o v e .*

For you were gone just
as soon as the waves touched
the shoreline —
everything we shared,
washing away,
sinking with the rest of us.

And here I am left
holding onto your shirts
the way that I wished to
hold onto you —
close to my heart;
wrapped around my naked body.

The Haunting

We were both wicked in our own
involuntary ways.
You, commanded by your demons
to enchant and then destroy me;
myself, filled with uncontrollable,
desire, and lust.

Yet you wished for your chance of
freedom, to *love* me.
and I wished to fight my sins,
to save you.

And I know that in the end
our souls will be faithful to
draw us up and out of this
wicked game that we have
for so long been forced to play.

The Haunting

It was this season
that I struggled to
hold onto what was left of
our warmth,
and so every winter
is now colder than it must be,
as I feel my heart
reenact its initial freeze.

The Haunting

There once was a time
where I had found myself
a prisoner to resentment,
and you feeding me through
my cell.

I was your bitter hostage,
desperate for an escape…
finally finding my pencil
to be the key, and my paper
to be the gate.

And then it became as clear as day to me,
that you were nothing more than a soul of
the world,
struggling to you *l o v e* yourself.

How might I expect you to muster
up the energy to in turn *l o v e*
someone else?

And that maybe I am to be the hero,
by simply praying for you and wishing you well.

Its an anorexic battle,
the way I hunger for *l o v e*
yet push the plate away.

Of all of the memories that I could leave
you with,
I have my heart set on the one of you
swiftly abandoning me —
the sound of the pain that was buried
deep within my silence,
and the devastation that was plastered
upon my pale and lifeless face.

I really don't much care to remind you
of the memories of all of the laughter
and romance that was once shared.

For as sure as the sun trades places
with the moon,
subconscious thoughts of this,
and of me,
will forever live inside of you.

The Haunting

It was when I learned that
no amount of bitterness, revenge,
or anger would avenge
the death of my soul,
after losing you—

that was, and I know
with full certainty, when I first
entered into the dark night of my soul.

To be left there,
without revenge as a weapon,
or rage as a wall to hide behind.

Bare, naked, and for the first time,
fully exposed…
a pure and broken heart,
irrevocably in *l o v e* with another,
who chose to walk away.

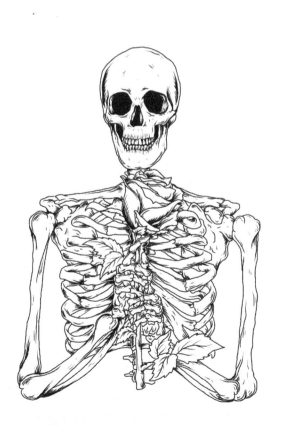

I was certain that I could live endless
days on this earth and still not understand
an ounce of it,
only my *l o v e* for him.

In your bed
where I used to lie,
project visions of me;
replace my spot,
never my memory.

It is the kind of *l o v e* that sends us rushing
to turn the pages of the former legends and
myths —
determined to find if even just
a fraction of an explanation as to what it is that
we are feeling.

The kind of *l o v e* that we find ourselves changing
for, seeking out patience, kindness,
and evolution of our soul for;
the kind of *l o v e* that we would risk it all for;
go to war for;
conquer the gates of hell for.

That is my *l o v e* for you.

The Haunting

The story of You and I
has always been one of
push and pull;
polarity in the form of
romance —
myself,
an angel,
and you,
an angel that fell long ago.

Or am I the fallen,
and you the risen?
Or at times, could it be that we
are both? —
Ever changing,
so that we might remain
opposites...
so that we might forever
and always,
attract.

And I've learned
this to be true,
that finding someone
you would endure
any amount of pain for
is mainly terrifying,
because in the long
list of possibilities
lie the most
excruciating of all—

that one day they
may decide to
up and leave.

Her arms wrapped firmly around him
was the equivalence of a pillow placed
over my head, robbing me of my very
breath;
a feeling that I could not fight;
a sight that I could no longer bare to see.

I grieve you as a death.
You are not something to be
grieved merely once,
or for an extended amount
of time,
but for the span of this lifetime.
Your memory is ever present,
with only fleeting moments of
distraction
to grace me a few vital
moments of relief.

I am not meant to move on,
I am meant to grieve.

The Haunting

My every thought tends
to rush its way out onto paper,
as blood gushing uncontrollably
from a fresh wound.

Here lie, as always, my feelings for you.

The Haunting

Oh
what it would be like
to live life as one of the heartless;
without a heart
on my sleeve,
or one to hand over
into the palm of another's
hand.

How I wish at times I
were one of the few.

How I wish I could set fire
to it all,
to finally rid myself of this
burden— *loving* you.

I've never *l o v e d* another
the way that I *l o v e* you,
for pushing me to my full potential;
for holding back in times
that I screamed for relief;
for helping me to finally bare witness
to my own strength;
for giving tough *l o v e* because of your
unwavering belief in me.

The Haunting

The memories of you and I
feel so distant, as if created in
a past life…
yet concurrently
close to me; penetrating all of me.

Its as if for some reason,
they wish to fight the hands of time,
living on, endlessly inside of me.
Awakening me.
Calling to me.
Longing for me.

In you,
I have placed in inconceivable
amount of pressure,
now I know.

To have made you my fortress,
knowing that in doing so I
was bypassing all of which
you desired for me to finally see —
that there had always been
something
larger than life
connecting you to me.

The Haunting

I see your chaos as beauty,
dark as it may be.

There is a kind of longing
where the misery begins to bring
forth a sense of peace.

Here lie the ashes of the poems…
the ones I wrote for you;
the ones you will never get to read.

Every vanishing word,
a critical role in setting
my heart free.

For wasn't it you that taught me
that there are hidden powers to our
every word?

Therefore,
with this truth,
I claim the power of them never being
heard.

The Haunting

My thoughts of you,
they never cease.
Like a fallen angel,
wishing to relinquish
their immortality
to escape their
never ending pain,
yet aware that this is
not their fate.

I cannot escape you.

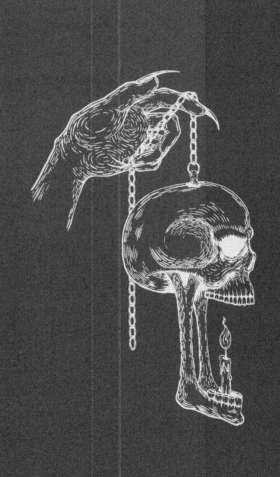

I have exhausted my efforts,
praying that I could simply move on from you.

I have tirelessly turned pages
in search of the answer,
bled onto blank pages of my own,
and chanted so hard that my
lungs begged me to hand back it's breath.

For now, I have no other choice
but to surrender and to rest.

The Haunting

I live in a world where it is
possible to meet the *l o v e*
of your life,
have them,
hold them,
and then to lose them.

I am an alien to this world,
lovesick, in search of my home.

I nearly drowned
when I felt you sinking —
willing to give my last breath
to help keep you afloat.

Kryptonite was once nothing more
than fiction to me —
something I had only read about
in comic books…
until my soul began to read yours.

I only began to crave all things
fire
having first
been burned by you.

I was so desiring of your touch,
that I was determined to run
after, face, and
build immunity to highest
degrees of heat.

I thought maybe I could
possibly learn to refine,
rather than melt,
if we were again, to meet.

The Haunting

The serpent mated with
the dove,
and from their bedroom
was born the most iconic
l o v e .

When it comes to you,
I overanalyze it all —
every word, ever facial expression,
every movement, or lack there of.
None of it ever meaningless;
all of it holding significance.

And that it what it is like
to be both hypersensitive and in *l o v e.*

Was it not enough that when you left,
you held hostage my heart.
You too had to take my sanity along with you?

The Haunting

Did I ever have a choice
to be anything other than resilient,
when it comes to you?

If I hadn't taken ahold of resiliency
and claimed it as mine,
I would have been driven mad
long ago.

Sometimes I hate that everything
about you is so cryptic, and that
I must always be a master decoder.

I wish you knew that you could bare your soul nude
and I'd still just as fervently *l o v e* you.

Another year has passed.

Another surge of increased
longing makes is way into me,
settling itself upon this raw
and wounded heart.

What have you done to me?

Time promised me healing,
yet here I am, walking backwards,
and thinking sideways.

It would be just like the universe
to place you into the strangers
walking past me on the street —
whether they have your stature,
your eyes,
or
your hair.

God damn this world for seeing
to it that you are nowhere,
yet seemingly everywhere all the same.

The Haunting

I've always desired more of you,
but all I've ever needed was some of you.

Its like baring my naked body to
all of the elements of this world —
hailstorms, tornadoes, fire and rain...
knowing that you, *my home,*
are currently the shelter of another.

The Haunting

You and I,
we are the fallen
leaves of Autumn.
Though the trees
have abandoned us,
happily we shall lie,
side by side.

You, the warmest
shade of orange,
and I,
as yellow as the
sun beaming down
from the sky.

Abandoned, yes.
Fallen, yes.
But beautiful,
and together —
and what a lovely way to die.

May you understand this
on your darkest day...

the haunting will soon be over,
and it is nothing more than a
purgatory to show us the way.

I hope you hold her every night the way
the way that you would hold me…
and then I hope that it haunts you.

That those deep breaths are no longer mine;
that the skin your fingers are tracing doesn't
encompass the soul that you were destined to *l o v e;*
that I am now left, freezing cold —
your hand, hidden from me,
nothing left for me to hold.

For forty days, and forty nights,
I wandered through the graveyard
of our memories.

There I whispered apologies into
dry stones,
and planted flowers of hope upon the
tombstones.
I prayed for a resurrection rooted
in absolute trust and forgiveness.

I prayed that though seven feet under,
l o v e was still holding on.

I imagine us to be magnets,
and the world,
fingers, harboring jealousy,
as they try their hardest to pry
us apart.

But they cannot keep apart
what is by law, meant to be.

L o v e
is
warm
and
ingenuous,
but it has
its moments
in time where
it too is paralyzing
and cold.

And the truth is,
I have never
experienced the
two hand in hand,
quite like I have with you.

I loved hard,
but I think I lost even harder.

With *l o v e* there are only two options,
it will either heal you or it will haunt you.

And to find out,
you must bravely take hold of it's hand.

The Haunting

In between rest and restlessness,
desire and fear,
I found you.

Lying in the shadows
with but a spec of light upon
my face,
it is here that I first felt you.

With your one horn and half
a halo, I embraced you.

And since then,
I have decided that I too am
neither an angel or a devil…
or perhaps I am the merging
of the two.

For whatever it is that you are,
it is this that I am as well.

The Haunting

If the days pass,
and the longing decreases,
it wasn't *l o v e ,*
it was a bruised ego.

If the the days pass,
and the longing increases,
it was *l o v e.*
It is *l o v e.*
It will always be *l o v e.*

He was both the taste of *l o v e* and of terror
on my tongue;
everlasting beauty and nightmare intricately
crossed with one another.
He was forever drawing me closer and closer to the death
of my former self,
yet life like I had only ever dreamt of.

The Haunting

If you cannot learn
to forgive,
you will die inside
of a body that is
still very much alive.

And that,
many claim,
is the most brutal
death of all.

Its *strange* isn't it?
That we would purposely
stick our fingers into
wounds on the verge
of healing,
just to feel them once more?

As an open wound is to hold blood,
a scar is to hold a memory.
Yet, unlike an open wound,
a scar knows far less pain.

And I feel that there is a
powerful message in that —
that no matter how loud your
wounds scream that this
is forever...
time reveals that the pain
is faithful to fade.

The Haunting

I suppose you *loving* me
was you leaving me —
subliminal messages hidden
within your goodbye,
telling me to first *love* myself.

The Haunting

I swallowed our encounter
as one would swallow the
red pill over the blue.

When you left,
I awakened as one would awaken
having survived a life threatening crash;
grogginess nearly over taking me,
yet enough awareness to feel the
weight of a body, bloody, beaten
and bruised.

Little did I then know,
I was awakening to a second chance
at life; a divine intervention —
mercy sparing me, while
guiding me to my heaven on earth.

In short,
you awakened me.
And though the awakening was
painful,
it gave birth to all that I would
ever need —
Belief.

ACKNOWLEDGEMENTS

My nameless lover, for awakening me to the depths.

God, for carrying me through the depths.

Myself, for being brave enough to follow.

My children, for being a positive focal point
on my hardest days.

My mother, my father, and my brother,
for supporting me in so many ways.

My readers, for sharing this journey and seeing
to it that I never feel alone.

I love you all so very much.

An acknowledgment from the author:

The cover art was illustrated by myself, the author.

All other illustrations found in this book have been obtained by various artists and have been purchased and licensed.

Thank you to all artists for helping me to create the aesthetic that I had always imagined for The Haunting. I am incredibly grateful for the way that each piece so perfectly tied this book together.

with all of my love,

-melissa m. combs

Made in the USA
Las Vegas, NV
10 December 2023

82461911R00125